Dragonflies
and Damselflies

TEXT BY ELAINE PASCOE

PHOTOGRAPHS BY DWIGHT KUHN

BLACKBIRCH PRESS
An imprint of Thomson Gale, a part of The Thomson Corporation

THOMSON
GALE

Detroit • New York • San Francisco • San Diego • New Haven, Conn. • Waterville, Maine • London • Munich

For more information, contact
Blackbirch Press
27500 Drake Rd.
Farmington Hills, MI 48331-3535
Or you can visit our Internet site at http://www.gale.com

Every effort has been made to trace the owners of copyrighted material.

Photo Credits: All photos © Dwight Kuhn

LIBRARY OF CONGRESS CATALOGING-IN-PUBLICATION DATA

Pascoe, Elaine.
  Dragonflies and damselflies / by Elaine Pascoe. Photographs by Dwight Kuhn.
    p. cm. — (Nature close-up)
  Includes bibliographical references (p.   ) and index.
  ISBN 1-56711-914-X (hardcover : alk. paper)
  1. Dragonflies—Juvenile literature. 2. Damselflies—Juvenile literature. I. Title.

  QL520.P37 2005
  595.7'33—dc22   2005005224

Printed in the United States of America
10 9 8 7 6 5 4 3 2 1

Contents

1

Dragons on the Wing

A flash of color darts through the warm summer air. It is a dragonfly, the flying ace of the insect world. Dragonflies zip across meadows and skim the surface of ponds. They can hover in midair, turn on a dime, and even fly backward! And with their shiny green, blue, and bronze colors, they are beautiful to watch.

With their large but delicate wings, dragonflies are fantastic fliers.

Dragonflies and their close relatives, damselflies, are fierce **predators**. They catch and eat other insects as they fly. Some tropical dragonflies are quite large, with a **wingspan** of more than 7 inches (18cm). Most kinds that live in North America are smaller, with wingspans measuring 2 to 3 inches (5 to 8cm). Still, they are big enough to startle you when they zoom past. Dragonflies frighten some people, but they are harmless. These fascinating insects are worth a closer look.

Fancy Fliers

Dragonflies and damselflies make up a big group of insects, with more than 5,100 different kinds worldwide. Some kinds have a wide range, but others are found in just a few places. You will most likely find them close to water of some kind—ponds, streams and rivers, or marshes.

These insects are easy to spot. They have long, thin bodies; long, transparent wings; and two huge eyes. Damselflies are generally smaller and slimmer than dragonflies, and there are a few other differences. But in most

Damselflies are smaller than dragonflies and do not fly as well.

ways the two groups are the same. Like all insects, they have a hard outer shell, or **exoskeleton**, instead of a bony inner skeleton. They have six legs and three main body parts—head, **thorax**, and abdomen.

The dragonfly's huge eyes take up most of its head. They are **compound eyes**, with almost 28,000 separate lenses. These eyes give the insect a wide field of vision, above, ahead, and to the sides. They are especially good at detecting movement. Two small antennae help the insect sense its world, but they are less important than the eyes.

A dragonfly's huge compound eyes allow it to look in all directions. Here you can also see the insect's two short antennae.

MAYFLIES: ALL IN A DAY

You can see many different kinds of insects flying around ponds and streams in warm weather. One type is the mayfly. Like dragonflies, mayflies are ancient insects. Their ancestors were probably among the first insects to fly.

Mayflies look a bit like dragonflies, but they are smaller—mostly less than $3/4$ inch (2cm) long. They have slender bodies and two pairs of wings. The front pair is usually much bigger than the hind pair.

Like dragonflies, mayflies begin their lives as nymphs in water. They breathe through gills and eat plants or other small water animals. They may spend

Mayflies spend most of their lives as nymphs like this one, living in freshwater streams and ponds.

up to three years as nymphs, growing and molting. Then they crawl out of the water and molt into winged adults. As nymphs and adults, mayflies are food for lots of other animals—including fish, frogs, birds, and hungry dragonflies.

Adult mayflies do not eat. They live only long enough to mate and lay eggs, sometimes just a day. Males form huge swarms, flying up and down a few feet above the ground. Females fly into the swarm to mate. Then they lay their eggs in streams and ponds. Their work done, the adults die.

An adult mayfly's life is short—sometimes just a day.

9

A dragonfly has a powerful pair of jaws, or **mandibles**. It also has a structure called a **labium**, which is something like a lower jaw. The dragonfly uses the labium to snag and hold its prey. It chews with the mandibles.

The dragonfly's legs are attached to the thorax, just behind the head. They point forward as the insect flies, ready to grab **prey**, and they are tipped with bristles that help the dragonfly hold on to what it catches. The dragonfly also uses its legs for perching, but it rarely walks.

The wings are also attached to the thorax. There are two pairs of wings. If you look closely, you will see that they are crisscrossed by veins, which provide support. There is a small notch on the front edge of each wing. In dragonflies, the rear wings are larger than the front wings. In damselflies, front and hind wings are similar in size.

Dragonflies are exceptional fliers. Some can hit speeds of 35 miles (56km) per hour. Damselflies are not as fast or strong in the air. While dragonflies zip and dart, damselflies flutter and dance. At rest, damselflies hold their wings up over their backs, like butterflies. Dragonflies keep their wings out to the side.

Both dragonflies and damselflies have a long, thin abdomen behind the thorax. The abdomen holds organs for reproduction and digestion.

Dragonflies and damselflies are big eaters, and they eat just about anything they can catch. Flies, mosquitoes, gnats, and other flying insects are their main prey. Dragonflies sometimes zoom through swarms of mayflies or other insects, scooping them up as they go. More often, they snatch their prey out of the air with their legs. But dragonflies do not hunt in cold weather and are often less active on cloudy days. Dameselflies are less sensitive to cold.

A dragonfly's wings are transparent and braced with veins. Its forelegs have bristles that help it catch prey.

Other animals, including birds, frogs, and spiders, sometimes eat dragonflies and damselflies. But with their keen eyes and flying skills, these insects are hard to catch.

Boy Meets Girl

Many kinds of male dragonflies are **territorial**. They stake out an area of a pond or stream and patrol it, driving other males away. Females usually stay away from the males until they are ready to mate and lay eggs.

A pair of dragonflies mating is really something to see. The male catches the female or lifts her into the air with his legs, holding her behind the head. As they fly, the female loops the end of her abdomen up to the base of the male's abdomen so that the two insects form a wheel. They mate while flying together this way. Damselflies, which do not fly as well, mate while perched on plants near the water.

After mating, the female lays her eggs. Different kinds of dragonflies and damselflies lay their eggs in different ways. Females of some types have a sharp organ called an ovipositor on their tail. They use it to cut into the

A garden spider uses silk to wrap up a dragonfly that blundered into its web.

stems of plants in or overhanging the water, and they lay their eggs in the plant stems. Females of other types lay their eggs directly in water. Sometimes the males fly along with the females as they lay their eggs.

A female may lay several batches of eggs over the course of a summer. Each batch may have a few hundred to a few thousand eggs, depending on the species. The eggs hatch anywhere from five days to several weeks later, depending on temperature and other conditions. Sometimes eggs laid late in summer do not hatch until the following spring.

Damselflies mate while clinging to plants. Inset: A dragonfly egg on the leaf of a water plant.

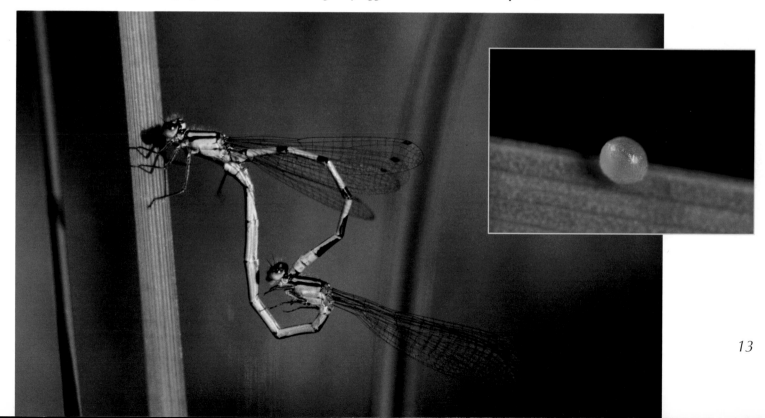

Life Underwater

The newly hatched insects are called **nymphs**. In looks and way of life, they are very different from adults. They live in the water, getting oxygen from the water through feathery organs called **gills**. You can see a damselfly nymph's gills at the end of its abdomen. A dragonfly nymph's gills are hidden inside its abdomen.

The nymphs' bodies are thicker than those of the adults. This is especially true for dragonfly nymphs. Their eyes are smaller, and they have no wings. While the adults are brightly colored, the nymphs are dull brown and olive green. But as predators, the nymphs are even fiercer than their parents. They ambush their prey.

A dragonfly nymph clings to a water plant, waiting for prey.

A nymph lies in wait for other water insects, worms, tadpoles, or small fish to swim by. Then it grabs its meal. The nymph has an amazing long labium that it keeps folded under its head most of the time. It can shoot the labium out in a flash to snatch prey. The nymph also defends itself with the labium, giving a little nip if it feels threatened.

Nymphs eat a lot and grow fast. But their exoskeletons do not grow. Like other young insects, a nymph must **molt** as it grows larger. It sheds its skin and steps out in a new, bigger skin. Nymphs spend anywhere from a year to six years in the water, molting as many as fifteen times. Their bodies change over time, becoming a little more like an adult with each molt.

The labium is tipped with sharp spines. The nymph can use it for defense as well as for hunting.

Above: The long labium of a dragonfly nymph can shoot forward to catch prey.

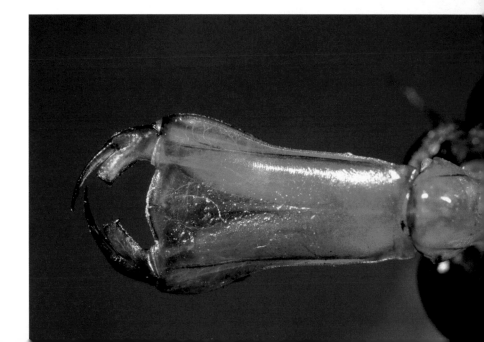

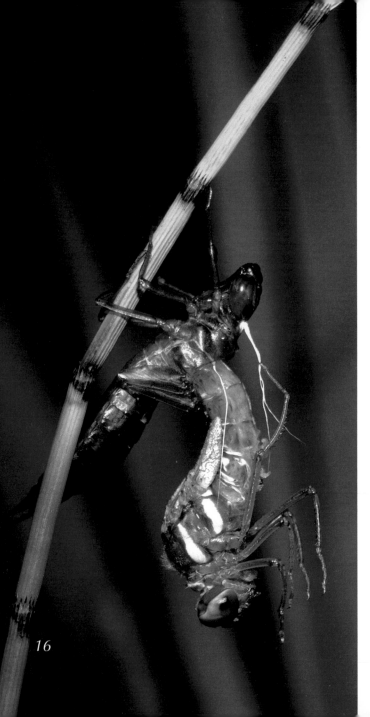

Finally the nymph crawls out of the water onto a rock or stem and prepares for its biggest change. It stops feeding and molts one last time, becoming a winged adult. Its body and wings are soft at first. But they quickly dry and stiffen, and the insect flies off to begin its adult life.

Dragonflies and damselflies actually spend most of their lives as nymphs in the water. As adults, they generally live just seven to ten weeks.

What's in a Name?

There are more than 500 different kinds of dragonflies and damselflies in North America. Each has a scientific name, in Latin. These scientific names allow scientists everywhere to identify an insect by the same name, no matter what language they speak. Dragonflies and damselflies also have common names, in English. Although common names can vary from place to place, they are the names that most people use. Here are the common names of six families.

An adult dragonfly crawls out of its old nymph skin.

16

- Clubtails have a bulge at the tip of the abdomen, so these dragonflies look like tiny flying clubs. The bulge is most noticeable in males.
- Cruisers zoom down the middle of streams and rivers. You may see one of these dragonflies tearing down the middle of a road at high speed, too.
- Darners are dragonflies that look like darning needles. A female darner lays her eggs in plant stems, pushing the tip of her abdomen into the stem like a needle.
- Emeralds are named for their beautiful coloring, generally metallic green or bronze. Most of these dragonflies also have bright green eyes. They are small to medium in size, with slender abdomens.

This elegant dragonfly is a black-tipped mosaic darner.

- Skimmers make up a big family found throughout much of North America. Skimmers include many different kinds of dragonflies. Most hunt by perching on twigs or rocks, scanning their surroundings for prey. A few fly almost nonstop during the day and even eat while flying. Females lay eggs directly in the water.
- Pond damsels are small blue and black damselfiies. They include bluets, dancers, and forktails. Most damselflies belong to this family.

Bluets like this one belong to the pond damselfly family. Inset: Skimmers are a large family of dragonflies.

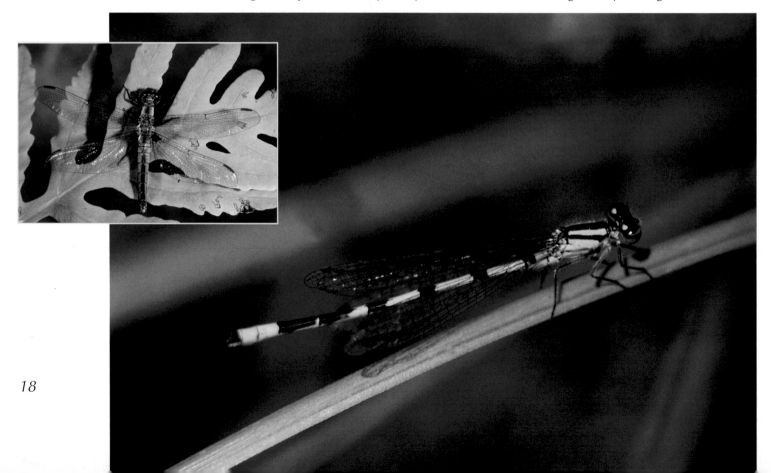

The ruby meadowhawk dragonfly is a member of the skimmer group.

Dragonflies help people by eating harmful insects like this female mosquito, seen sucking blood from a person.

Dragonflies and People

Dragonflies and damselflies are **beneficial** insects. They help people by eating mosquitoes and other pests. But people have had lots of strange beliefs about dragonflies over the years.

In Europe, people used to think that dragonflies were harmful or evil. They called the insects "horse stingers" or "devil's darning needles." One old superstition was that dragonflies would stitch shut the mouths of children who told lies. But in Japan dragonflies are honored symbols of happiness, strength, and success. They are also used in the traditional medicine of Japan and China. And they are on the menu, fried or in soup, in Indonesia and in parts of Africa and South America.

Some dragonflies are quite rare. One, the Hine's emerald dragonfly, is listed as an **endangered species**. This small green insect is found only in a handful of places in Wisconsin and Illinois. Most dragonflies are not endangered, but they do face threats. When people fill in marshes and ponds for development, they destroy the **habitat** of these insects. And many dragonflies are very sensitive to pollution. If you see a lot of dragonflies at a pond or a marsh, that is a good sign that the water is clean.

Older Than Dinosaurs

Dragonflies are among the most ancient insects. Ancestors of today's dragonflies flew through prehistoric forests 325 million years ago. That's about 125 million years before the first dinosaurs appeared! These dragonfly ancestors were giants, with wingspans of 30 inches (75cm). When the dinosaurs died out, about 65 million years ago, the dragonflies remained. They looked pretty much the same as the dragonflies of today.

2

Collecting and Caring for Dragonflies

Dragonflies are fun to watch as they dart and hover in the sunlight. The adult insects are hard to catch and even harder to keep for study, however. They need room to roam and flying insects to eat.

Nymphs are much easier to care for. You can order dragonfly nymphs from biological supply companies such as those listed on page 44. If you live near a pond, you can find your own nymphs. This chapter will tell you how to collect and care for them. Keep them for just a short time, and then return them to the place where you found them.

Equipment for Collecting

To gather dragonfly nymphs, you will need a long-handled collection net and a container in which to carry the nymphs home. You can buy a collection net, but it is easy to make one.

What to Do:

• If you use a food strainer, tape it tightly to the mop handle. If you use a mesh laundry bag, do this:

1. Bend the clothes hanger to form a round loop. Straighten the hanger's hook.

2. Put the open end of the bag through the loop, so that it forms a pouch about 12 inches (30 cm) deep.

3. Fold the open end back over the wire loop, and sew it in place.

4. Tape the net to the handle.

Your container can be any sort of wide-mouthed plastic pail or jar. It should have a lid or be deep enough to keep water from slopping out when you carry it. Fill the container with pond water at the collecting site.

What You Need:
• Mop or broom handle
• Black electrical tape
• Large food strainer or mesh laundry bag.
If you use the bag, you will also need:
• Clothes hanger
• Needle and thread

You may also find it helpful to bring along a shallow, light-colored container such as a plastic dishpan or an old food keeper. If you empty your net into the flat pan first, you will be able to see and sort out debris and water animals that you do not want. Then you can put only the material you do want into your collecting jar.

Where and How to Search

Look for dragonfly larvae during warm weather in shallow, quiet freshwater. The edges of ponds and marshes are good places to search. When you visit a pond or marsh, take an adult with you. Follow these steps for safety:
- Wear old sneakers or sandals for wading. Do not go barefoot because glass or sharp stones may be hidden under the water.
- Use your net handle or another pole to test the depth of the water ahead of you, to be sure that the bottom does not drop off suddenly.
- Avoid streams with fast-running currents. They can be dangerous, and you are less likely to find nymphs there.
- Do not hunt for nymphs by leaning from a boat or dock—you might fall into deep water.

Nymphs often lurk where water plants grow. They are hard to see, but if you sweep your net through the water in these areas you may catch some. Do not pick up the nymphs with your hands—they can nip.

The edge of a pond or marsh is a good place to hunt for dragonfly nymphs.

Collect just a few. Remember that the nymphs are predators. If you put large nymphs in a container with small nymphs or other water animals, the large nymphs will eat them.

Put some pond plants in your container with the nymphs. To make sure the nymphs get home safely, cover the container only when you are carrying it. Otherwise, leave it open so that air can reach the water surface.

A small aquarium with a few water plants is a good home for nymphs.

Caring for Dragonfly Nymphs

At home, set up a small aquarium for your nymphs. Put clean sand or gravel in the bottom. Then fill the aquarium half full with pond water or with tap water that is free of chlorine. You can remove chlorine by letting the water stand in an open container for 24 hours, or by using a chemical that you can buy at a pet store.

Put some plants in the aquarium, too. You can use pond plants or water plants from a pet store. The plants will give the nymphs places to crawl around and hide. To keep the plants healthy, you will need to place the container in bright light. But do not put it in direct sunlight, which could overheat the water and harm the nymphs.

A dragonfly nymph (above) will need a steady supply of live prey, such as small guppies (below).

The water should be at room temperature before you add the nymphs. Use a spoon or a small aquarium net to move them into their new home.

You will need to feed your nymphs live prey. The prey can be small tropical fish, such as guppies, or critters you catch in the pond—small tadpoles, aquatic insects, and minnows. Prey should be the same size or smaller than the nymphs. You will have to provide a continuous supply of food, or the nymphs may eat each other.

An adult dragonfly dries its wings after its final molt.

Nymphs will eventually turn into winged adults. This may not happen for a year or more, so you may never see it happen. But you should prepare for it by placing some sticks or plant stems in the aquarium, with their tops out of the water.

This will give the nymphs a dry place for their final molt. Cover the top of the aquarium with netting, so you can capture the adults. After you have had a chance to see them, let them go.

Leaves and twigs that extend up from the water will give your nymphs a place to make their final molt.

29

3

Investigating Dragonflies

In this chapter, you will find projects and activities that will help you learn more about dragonflies and damselflies. The projects can be done with nymphs that you have collected or ordered through the mail. Have fun with these activities. Remember to use an aquarium net or a spoon to move the nymphs, as they may bite. When you are done, return any insects you have collected to the places where you found them. Insects that you have ordered through the mail should not be released.

Do Dragonfly Nymphs Prefer Open Water or Water with Lots of Plants?

What You Need:
- Small glass or clear plastic container or aquarium
- Clean sand or gravel
- Pond water or tap water treated to remove chlorine
- Water plants
- Dragonfly nymph

Dragonfly nymphs live in many freshwater habitats—ponds, lakes, marshes, and slow-running streams. Do they swim mainly in open water or stay among water plants? Decide what you think, based on what you have read about these insects. Then do this activity to see if you are right.

What to Do:

1. Set up the container as described in chapter 2.

2. Anchor the water plants in the sand or gravel in one-half of the container. Leave the other half without plants.

3. Put the nymph in the container.

4. Check the container several times to see where the nymph is.

Results: Where does the nymph spend most of its time, among the plants or in the open water?

Conclusion: What do your results tell you about the kind of habitat dragonfly nymphs prefer? How do you think this habitat helps them survive?

What Kinds of Prey Do Dragonfly Nymphs Prefer?

Given a choice, what do you think dragonfly nymphs would like to see on their menu? Make your best guess. Then do this project to find out.

What to Do:

1. Add several kinds of prey to your aquarium. You can use water insects, small fish, tadpoles, salamander larvae, or water snails. The prey should be smaller than the nymphs. Try to get prey that is all about the same size.

2. Watch to see what the nymphs do.

Results: Did the nymphs seem to go for one type of prey over another? Were there any types that they did not like? Or did they just grab the nearest prey? Try the activity again with different prey, and see if you get the same results.

Conclusion: What do your results show about the feeding habits of dragonfly nymphs?

Tadpoles are among many kinds of prey that dragonfly nymphs eat in the wild.

A skimmer dragonfly nymph.

Do Dragonfly Nymphs Prefer Shade or Bright Light?

Adult dragonflies are active during the day and like bright sunlight best. Do the nymphs share the adults' fondness for light? Decide what you think, and then do this activity.

What to Do:

1. Fill the container with pond water or treated tap water.

2. Place the nymph in the water, using a spoon.

3. Cover half of the container with a dark cloth. Leave the other side uncovered, in bright light.

4. Watch to see what the nymph does.

Results: Where does the nymph spend the most time? Try the activity with a different nymph, and see if you get the same results.

Conclusion: Based on your results, do you think the nymphs prefer shade or light?

What You Need:
- Flat container
- Pond water or tap water treated to remove chlorine
- Dark cloth
- Spoon
- Dragonfly nymph

What You Need:
- Two containers, both the same size
- Pond water or tap water treated to remove chlorine
- Water plants
- Two dragonfly nymphs, both the same size
- Spoon
- Small prey such as guppies, all the same size

Will Plants Help Prey Escape Dragonfly Nymphs?

Dragonfly nymphs are great hunters. Can small fish and other prey escape the nymphs by hiding in water plants? Based on what you know about the nymphs, make your best guess. Then do this experiment to see if you are right.

Can you spot the prey in the jar with more plants? Will the nymph find it?

What to Do:

1. Fill the containers with pond water or treated water.

2. Put a few water plants in one container. Put lots of water plants in the other.

3. Place a dragonfly nymph in each container, using a spoon.

4. Add an equal number of prey animals to each container. They should all be the same kind and size. You can buy guppies from a pet store for this.

5. Check the containers often to see how many guppies remain.

Use a spoon to move dragonfly nymphs.

Results: Which container ran out of guppies first?

Conclusion: Did the plants help the guppies or not?

More Activities with Dragonflies and Damselflies

1. Watch dragonflies and damselflies at a pond or swamp. How much time do they spend in the air, and how much time perching? Do they come back to the same perch after a flight? Do they fly mostly over water or over land? How high do they go? What patterns do they make in the air? Keep a notebook of your observations.

A banded-winged meadowhawk, a member of the skimmer family.

A dragonfly nymph eats a tadpole.

2. Compare dragonflies and damselflies that you see in the wild. See if you can find different kinds of each. How do they differ in size and shape? How do they hold their wings at rest? How do their flights compare?

3. Watch a dragonfly nymph eat. How does it hold its prey? How does it chew? Does it eat the whole animal, or are there leftovers? How long does it take to finish its meal?

4. See how a dragonfly nymph reacts to a threat. If you lower a pencil or similar object toward a nymph, does it move forward, backward, or to the side? Quickly or slowly? What does the nymph do if you put an object between it and its prey?

Results and Conclusions

Here are some possible results and conclusions for the activities on pages 31 to 37. Many factors may affect the results of these activities. If your results differ, try to think of reasons why. Repeat the activity with different conditions, and see if your results change.

Do dragonfly nymphs prefer open water or water with lots of plants?
The nymphs will probably spend more time among the plants. Their dull, mottled colors blend in with the colors of the plants. In the wild, this helps them hide and ambush their prey.

What kinds of prey do dragonfly nymphs prefer?
Our nymphs were not picky eaters. They went for anything that moved. They did not try to eat snails, perhaps because of the snails' shells.

Do dragonfly nymphs prefer shade or bright light?
Our nymphs did not prefer one side of the container over the other. Light is probably not as important to the nymphs as it is to adult dragonflies.

Will plants help prey escape dragonfly nymphs?
Guppies will probably survive longer in the container with more plants. The plants give the fish places to hide from the dragonfly nymphs.

Some Words About Dragonflies and Damselflies

beneficial Helpful.

compound eyes Eyes that have many lenses, or facets.

endangered species An animal or plant that is in danger of dying out.

exoskeleton The hard outer skin of an insect. It takes the place of an internal skeleton.

gills Organs that allow water-dwelling animals to get oxygen from water.

habitat The place where an animal or plant naturally lives.

labium A structure like a lower jaw that dragonflies and damselflies use to catch and hold prey.

mandibles The jaws of dragonflies and certain other insects.

molt Shed the skin or outer covering.

nymphs Immature forms of certain insects. Nymphs often look like adults without wings.

predators Animals that kill and eat other animals.

prey An animal that is caught and eaten by another animal.

territorial Defending a fixed area, or territory, from others.

thorax The center section of an insect's body. Usually the legs and wings are attached here.

wingspan The distance from the tip of one outstretched wing to the tip of the opposite wing.

Sources for *Dragonfly Nymphs*

You can buy dragonfly nymphs through mail-order sources such as these.

Carolina Biological Supply Company
2700 York Road
Burlington, NC 27215
(800) 334-5551
www.carolina.com

Connecticut Valley Biological Supply
82 Valley Road
PO Box 326
Southampton, MA 01073
(800) 628-7748
www.ctvalleybio.com

For More Information

Books

Kelly L. Borchelt, *Dragonfly*. San Diego, CA: Kidhaven Press, 2004.

Discovery Channel Science, *Insects*. Milwaukee, WI: Gareth Stevens, 2002.

Liza Jacobs, *Dragonflies*. San Diego, CA: Blackbirch Press, 2003.

Sally Kneidel, *More Pet Bugs: A Kid's Guide to Catching and Keeping Insects and Other Small Creatures*. Hoboken, NJ: John Wiley & Sons 1999.

Kristin Joy Pratt-Serafini, *Salamander Rain: A Lake & Pond Journal*. Nevada City, CA: DAWN, 2001.

Christina Wilsdon, *Insects (National Audubon Society First Field Guides)*. New York: Scholastic, 1998.

Web Site

Dragonflies and Damselflies of the United States (www.npwrc.usgs.gov/resource/distr/insects/dfly/dflyusa.htm). Find out what dragonflies and damselflies live near you.

Index